I love dinosaurs

priddy books
big ideas for little people

DO NOT EVER look inside T-rex's mouth when OPEN WIDE

Tyrannosaurus rex

"CRASH"

"STOMP"

GIANT
MEAT EATERS

Looking for a TASTY TREAT,
Allosaurus found some MEAT

"Roar!"

Allosaurus

Carnotaurus
with scaly bumps
on its back,
this dino HUNTED
in a pack

vicious

nimble

jaw

SMALL meat eaters

Deinonychus

had jaws **a-SNAPPING**, teeth bared and **SHARP** claws slashing

Archaeopteryx

A DINOSAUR?

why how **ABSURD!** This creature was quite like a bird

Velociraptor was VERY *quick*, with **big** sharp teeth and a killer KICK!

Troodon hunted **night and** day, eating EVERYTHING in his way

Gentle giants

Diplodocus

"plod" "plod"

Apatosaurus could reach the **trees**, for tasty twigs AND yummy **leaves**

Walking **S-L-O-W-L-Y** on all **fours,** these were the **LARGEST** dinosaurs

"I am very very l-o-n-g"

Brachiosaurus

Extremely l-o-n-g from top to toe, this dinosaur lived LONG AGO...

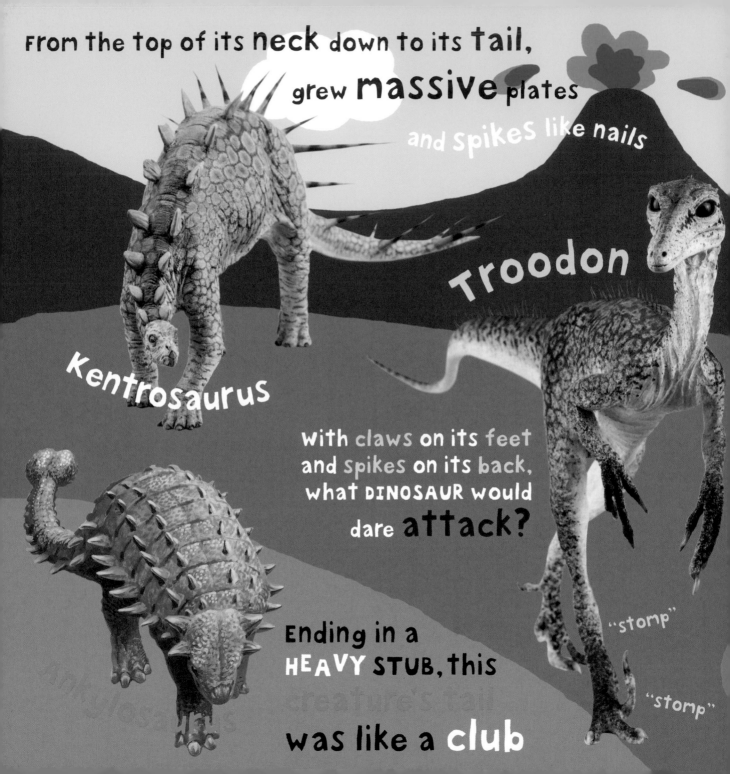

This dinosaur would swing its **tail** to **FIGHT** another **armored** male

Euoplocephalus

"smack!"

"ouch!"

Plates and Spikes

STEGOSAURUS was very **tall**,

"My brain is really tiny!"

his body was **BIG** but his brain was SMALL

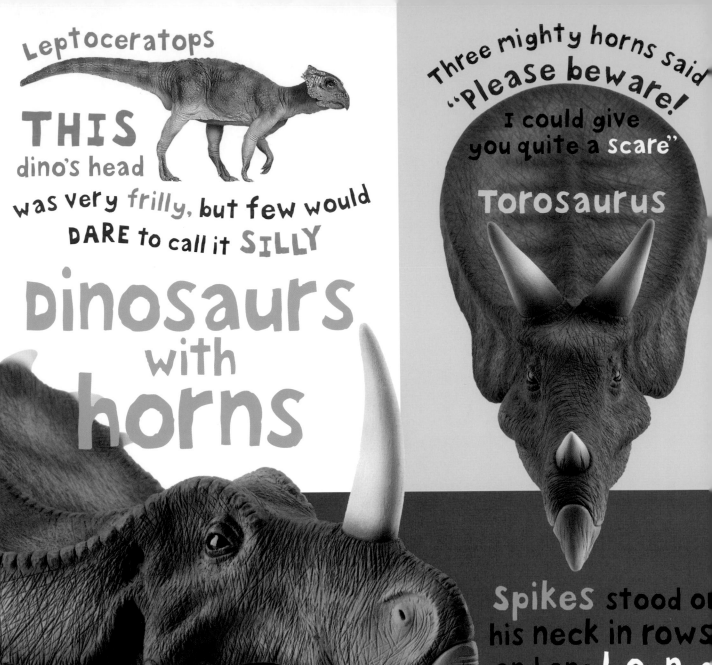

Leptoceratops

THIS dino's head was very frilly, but few would DARE to call it SILLY

Dinosaurs with horns

Three mighty horns said "Please beware! I could give you quite a scare"

Torosaurus

STYRACOSAURUS

Spikes stood on his neck in rows and one l-o-n-g HORN grew on his nose

Chasmosaurus

This armored **beast** did not eat meat, **BUT** SEARCHED for grass on his **four big feet!**

"using our horns to **charge** and **fight**, we were a very FEARSOME sight!"

Triceratops

's this the DINOSAUR I SEEK,
with two **strong** legs
and a pointed beak?

Ornithominus

Fabrosaurus

choosing
plants to eat for lunch,
there's nothing better-
"Munch, Munch,
MUNCH!!"

small
and
speedy

Speeeeding fast along
the ground,
whirling, *zooming,*
round and round

Zephyrosaurus

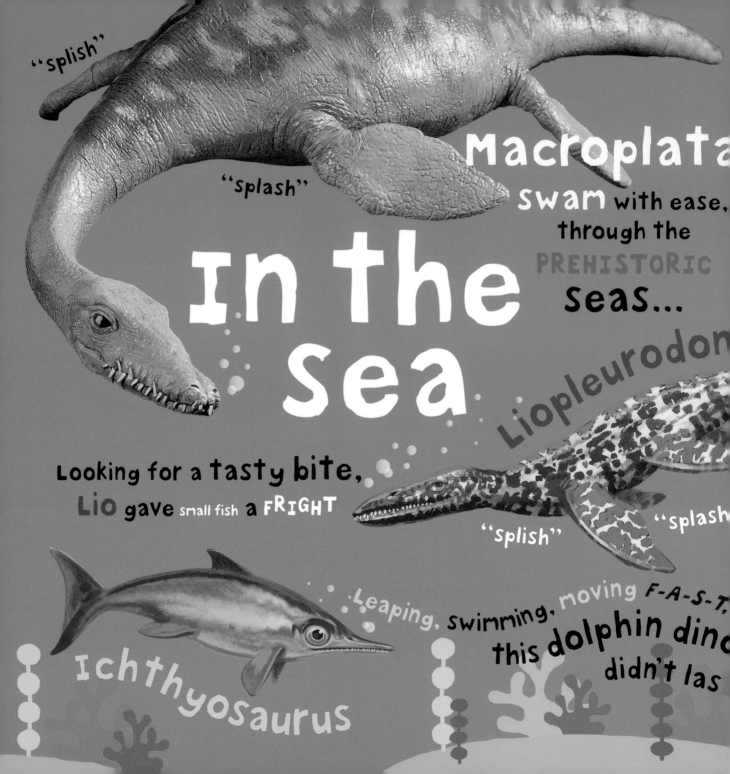

"splish"

"splash"

In the Sea

Macroplata
swam with ease,
through the
PREHISTORIC
Seas...

Liopleurodon

Looking for a tasty bite,
Lio gave small fish a FRIGHT

"splish"

"splash

Leaping, swimming, moving F-A-S-T,
this **dolphin dino** didn't las

Ichthyosaurus

Pteranodon

flew through the SKY,
its leathery wings
helped it FLY

Dimorphodon

No bird on EARTH looks like this,
but this flying creature
did exist!

In the air

Try this FUNNY little game-
say this flying
creature's name!
Quetzalcoatlus

"whish"

"whoosh"

Record breakers

Brachiosaurus wins a prize, for his **monumental** size

1st

"I'm the **KING** of the sky, the biggest creature ever to fly!"

biggest flying creature!

1st

Quetzalcoatlus

e couldn't run quite like the rest, but **his** armor was the best!

BEST body armor

Euoplocephalus

MOST FIERCE!

Many dinosaurs took **fright** when **carnotaurus** came in sight

FINISH

rnithomimus **wins first place** **n a dino running race**

FASTEST

Diplodocus is very long,
his neck and tail go on and on...

High and low

Flying, gliding, soaring high, **Pteranodon** races **through the sky**

Thud, crash, thump on the forest floor

Galliminus s small and *fast,* zoom, whizz, **Whoosh!** e dashes past

Watch out for Brachiosaurus- the **massive** dinosaur!

Parasaurolophus

Which dinosaur do you most dread?
One like this with a
strange-shaped head?

Corythosaurus

Look at him! His crest's so cool.
We don't know how he used
this tool! Do you?

Funny dino heads

Homalocephale

Using it to bruise and batter,
this one's head was slightly flatter

Stegoceras

Life was NEVER ever dull
for a dino with a bony skull!